Celebrity Bios

BAD BUNNY

Rebecca Rowell

WWW.APEXEDITIONS.COM

Copyright © 2025 by Apex Editions, Mendota Heights, MN 55120. All rights reserved. No part of this book may be reproduced or utilized in any form or by any means without written permission from the publisher.

Apex is distributed by North Star Editions:
sales@northstareditions.com | 888-417-0195

Produced for Apex by Red Line Editorial.

Photographs ©: Owen Sweeney/Invision/AP Images, cover, 1; Timothy Norris/FilmMagic/Getty Images, 4–5; Chris Pizzello/Invision/AP Images, 6–7, 24–25; Shutterstock Images, 8–9, 10–11, 12–13, 18–19, 20–21, 22–23, 27, 28–29, 36–37, 49, 52–53, 58; iStockphoto, 14–15; Gladys Vega/WireImage/Getty Images, 16–17; Kevin Winter/Getty Images Entertainment/Getty Images, 30–31, 38–39; Kevin Mazur/Getty Images Entertainment/Getty Images, 32–33; Kevin Winter/BBMA2020/Getty Images Entertainment/Getty Images, 34–35; Johnny Nunez/Getty Images Entertainment/Getty Images, 40–41; Steve Jennings/Getty Images Entertainment/Getty Images, 42–43; Frazer Harrison/Getty Images Entertainment/Getty Images, 44–45; Taylor Hill/Getty Images Entertainment/Getty Images, 46–47; Jason Koerner/Getty Images Entertainment/Getty Images, 50–51; Alejandro Granadillo/AP Images, 54–55; Randy Shropshire/Getty Images Entertainment/Getty Images, 56–57

Library of Congress Control Number: 2023922372

ISBN
979-8-89250-215-3 (hardcover)
979-8-89250-236-8 (paperback)
979-8-89250-276-4 (ebook pdf)
979-8-89250-257-3 (hosted ebook)

Printed in the United States of America
Mankato, MN
082024

NOTE TO PARENTS AND EDUCATORS

Apex books are designed to build literacy skills in striving readers. Exciting, high-interest content attracts and holds readers' attention. The text is carefully leveled to allow students to achieve success quickly.

TABLE OF CONTENTS

Chapter 1
AT THE GRAMMYS 4

Chapter 2
EARLY LIFE 8

Chapter 3
FOCUSING ON MUSIC 16

In the Spotlight
KING OF LATIN TRAP 26

Chapter 4
RISING HIGHER 28

Chapter 5
SUPERSTAR 38

In the Spotlight
SOUNDS OF HOME 48

Chapter 6
MANY SUCCESSES 50

FAST FACTS • 59
COMPREHENSION QUESTIONS • 60
GLOSSARY • 62
TO LEARN MORE • 63
ABOUT THE AUTHOR • 63
INDEX • 64

Chapter 1

AT THE GRAMMYS

Bad Bunny stands onstage. He begins rapping. A huge crowd sits in front of him. Millions of people also watch on TV. He is the opening act of the 2023 Grammy Awards.

More than 12.5 million viewers watched the 2023 Grammy Awards broadcast.

Bad Bunny raps in Spanish. He walks through the audience. Dancers follow him. Some are dressed in bright colors. Others wear large headpieces. People in the audience sing and dance along.

A BIG EVENT

The Grammys are important awards in music. People in the industry vote for the winners. Winning a Grammy is a big honor. So is performing at the awards show. The 2023 show was a milestone. It was the first to open with an all-Spanish performance.

The papier-mâché figures in Bad Bunny's performance represented famous Puerto Ricans through history.

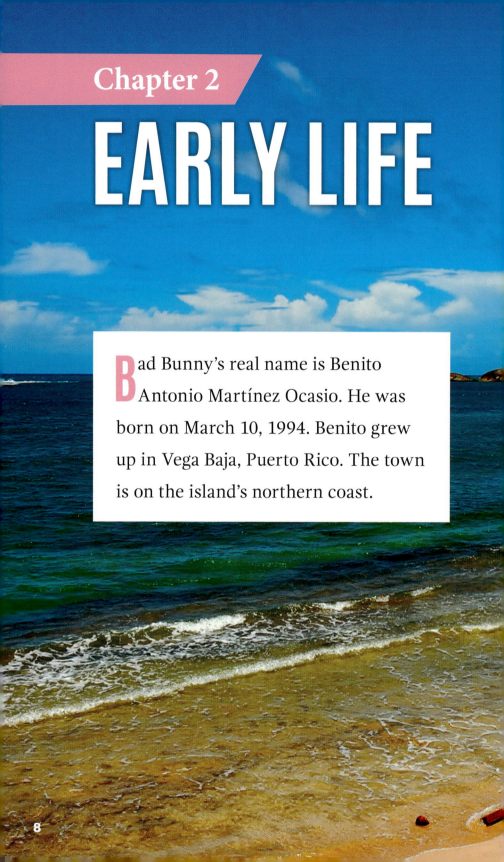

Chapter 2
EARLY LIFE

Bad Bunny's real name is Benito Antonio Martínez Ocasio. He was born on March 10, 1994. Benito grew up in Vega Baja, Puerto Rico. The town is on the island's northern coast.

Benito grew up close to beaches in Vega Baja, Puerto Rico.

Benito grew up with his parents and brothers. His father was a truck driver. His mother was an English teacher. Benito's mom loved salsa music. On weekends, she played music while cleaning. Sometimes Benito helped. He listened to her favorite singers.

MUSIC ALL AROUND

Benito's family was Catholic. They attended church services. When Benito was five, he joined his church's choir. He sang in the choir until he was 13.

Salsa dancing often goes along with salsa music. The dance style is popular in many parts of Latin America.

Benito listened to other music styles, too. Reggaeton was one of his favorites. He also listened to merengue and rock. As a teen, he started creating his own music. He came up with beats and raps. He freestyled for his classmates. Then he started putting his music online. He released some songs on SoundCloud.

SOUNDCLOUD

SoundCloud is a music website. Artists can share their music. Listeners can post their thoughts, too. The platform helps many artists launch their careers. They can find audiences. And they can get feedback.

Merengue music often features percussion instruments such as the guira (left) and tambora (right).

Benito attended college in Arecibo, Puerto Rico.

After high school, Benito went to college. He earned money by working at a grocery store. But he also kept making music. He put more songs on SoundCloud. In 2016, his song "Diles" ("Tell Them") became a hit. Suddenly, record labels wanted to sign him. Other musicians wanted to work with him, too. The song changed Benito's life.

PICKING A NAME

Benito had a childhood photo of himself in a bunny costume. That's where he got the name Bad Bunny. He posted the photo online. He thought people would like the name. He thought they would remember it, too.

15

Chapter 3
FOCUSING ON MUSIC

Bad Bunny's music was taking off. So, he found a manager. They planned to post more of his music online. Soon, he signed with a record label. It was run by DJ Luian. He was a famous reggaeton musician. Bad Bunny stopped going to college. He wanted to focus on music.

In late 2016, Bad Bunny (left) sang onstage with Latin music star Maluma.

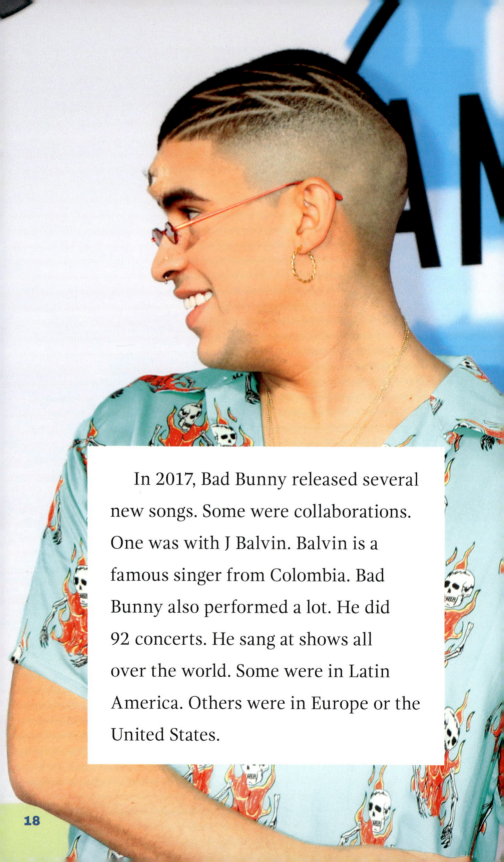

In 2017, Bad Bunny released several new songs. Some were collaborations. One was with J Balvin. Balvin is a famous singer from Colombia. Bad Bunny also performed a lot. He did 92 concerts. He sang at shows all over the world. Some were in Latin America. Others were in Europe or the United States.

> In 2018, Bad Bunny (left) and J Balvin attended the American Music Awards.

FIRST US TOUR

Bad Bunny's first full US tour was in 2018. He didn't have an album yet. But he performed his hit singles. He performed collaborations, too. The tour was a success. It made at least $16 million.

19

In 2018, Bad Bunny collaborated again. He worked with J Balvin and Cardi B. Their song was called "I Like It." It hit No. 1 in the United States. Bad Bunny also made a song with Drake in 2018. It was called "Mia." It reached No. 5. Those songs added to Bad Bunny's fame.

CARDI B

Cardi B is an American rapper. She was born in 1992 in New York City. Her mother is from Trinidad. Her father is from the Dominican Republic. Like Bad Bunny, her first language was Spanish.

Cardi B performed at Global Citizen Festival in New York in 2018.

Bad Bunny performed during the 92nd Annual Macy's Thanksgiving Day Parade in 2018.

Later in 2018, Bad Bunny released his first album. It was called *X 100PRE*. The title means "Forever." The songs included many types of Latin music. The album was a massive hit. People across the world loved it. In just a few months, the album sold 10 million copies.

SURPRISE ALBUM

In June 2019, Bad Bunny and J Balvin surprised fans. They released a new album, *Oasis*. The project had been a secret. Fans were excited. Critics were, too. The album earned a Grammy nomination.

X 100PRE won a Latin Grammy Award in 2019.

In 2019, Bad Bunny earned several award nominations. They were for the Latin American Music Awards. One was Artist of the Year. Others were Song of the Year and Album of the Year. Bad Bunny didn't win. However, it was still an honor. People were noticing his talent.

In the Spotlight

KING OF LATIN TRAP

Bad Bunny is sometimes known as the "King of Latin Trap." Latin trap is a type of hip-hop. It combines reggaeton and Southern rap. The lyrics are in Spanish.

Latin trap began in Puerto Rico. "El Pistolón" was the first song in this style. It came out in 2007. It featured several artists. They included Arcángel and De La Ghetto. In 2016, De La Ghetto released "La Ocasión." This song helped Latin trap grow. It featured Anuel AA, Arcángel, and Ozuna. All became big stars.

De La Ghetto attends the Latin American Music Awards in 2015.

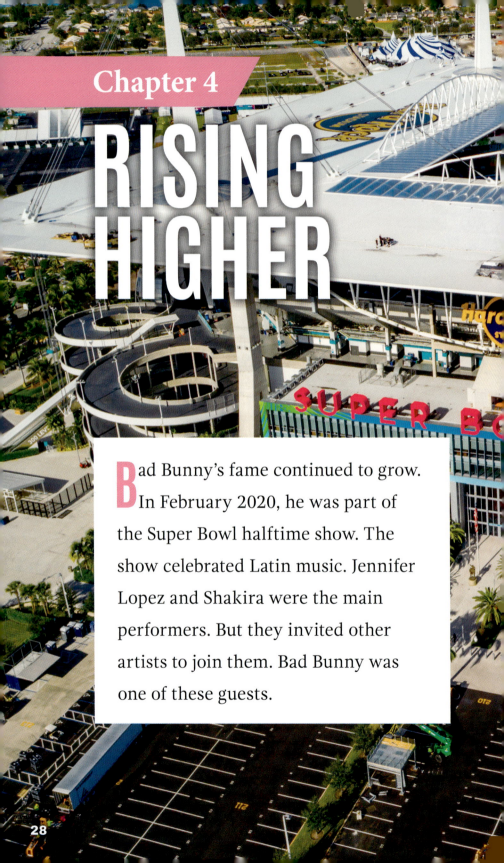

Chapter 4
RISING HIGHER

Bad Bunny's fame continued to grow. In February 2020, he was part of the Super Bowl halftime show. The show celebrated Latin music. Jennifer Lopez and Shakira were the main performers. But they invited other artists to join them. Bad Bunny was one of these guests.

Super Bowl LIV was played near Miami, Florida. More than 100 million people watched Bad Bunny perform on TV.

Bad Bunny won a Grammy for *YHLQMDLG*.

Later that month, Bad Bunny released an album. He titled it *YHLQMDLG*. That stood for "Yo hago lo que me da la gana." That means "I do what I want." The album did well on both Latin and US charts. Bad Bunny's audience was growing and growing.

In May 2020, Bad Bunny already had another album ready. It was called *Las Que No Iban a Salir*. That means "The Ones That Weren't Coming Out." This album had songs he made while working on other projects.

STICKING WITH SPANISH

Bad Bunny sings in Spanish. He usually speaks Spanish, too. That includes speeches at awards shows. Some people think he could reach more listeners by using English. In the past, some stars made that change. Bad Bunny chose not to. He wants to stay true to himself.

In October 2020, Bad Bunny performed at a show for singer Rihanna's brand Fenty.

Bad Bunny performed at the Billboard Music Awards in October 2020.

In November 2020, Bad Bunny released *El Último Tour del Mundo*. Its title means "The Last World Tour." This album earned him a huge achievement. It topped the Billboard 200 album chart. No all-Spanish album had ever done this before.

Bad Bunny rehearses for a show. Live performances are important to him.

36

That same year, Bad Bunny won a Latin Grammy for Best Reggaeton Performance. He also set streaming records. He was Spotify's most-streamed artist in 2020. That was a first for a Spanish-language artist. And *YHLQMDLG* was the most-streamed album on Spotify that year. It got more than 3.3 billion streams.

PERFORMING ONLINE

In 2020, the COVID-19 pandemic was happening. To try to slow its spread, many events were canceled. Artists couldn't do shows in person. So, Bad Bunny did his first online concert. More than 10 million people watched live.

Chapter 5
SUPERSTAR

In 2022, Bad Bunny released *Un Verano Sin Ti*. That title means "A Summer Without You." The album topped the Billboard 200 album chart. It also won several awards. One was the Global Album Award. The award tracks the top-selling albums in the world. Bad Bunny was the first Latin American artist to win it.

Bad Bunny's concerts often include colorful outfits and bright props.

Un Verano Sin Ti won the Grammy Award for Best Música Urbana Album.

Bad Bunny made history at the Grammys as well. *Un Verano Sin Ti* was up for the biggest award, Album of the Year. Until then, no Spanish-language album had been nominated. Bad Bunny didn't win. Still, the nomination was important. It showed that Latin music was mainstream in the United States.

RICKY MARTIN

Past Latin artists also helped make Latin music popular in the United States. In 1999, Ricky Martin performed at the Grammys. Martin's song "Livin' La Vida Loca" reached No. 1. In 2019, Martin released "Cántalo." Bad Bunny joined him on the song.

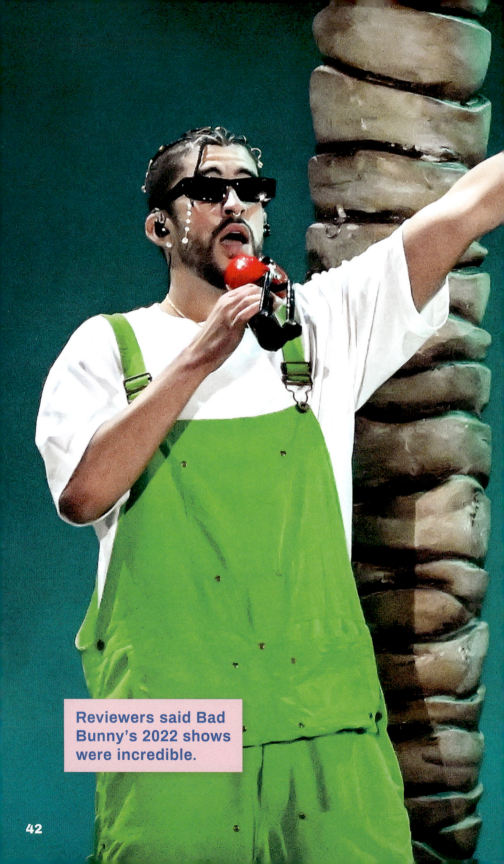

Reviewers said Bad Bunny's 2022 shows were incredible.

Bad Bunny also performed 81 concerts in 2022. The shows were part of two huge tours. These tours were a big success. In total, Bad Bunny made more than $435 million in ticket sales. That set a new record. It was the most money earned by an artist in one year.

In 2023, Bad Bunny made history again. He headlined Coachella with BLACKPINK and Frank Ocean. Coachella is a huge music festival. Bad Bunny was its first Latin headliner. Other Spanish-language artists performed, too. They included Becky G and Rosalía.

COACHELLA

Coachella began in 1999. It takes place over a few days in California each year. Musicians from many styles perform. The event attracts a huge audience. More than 500,000 people came in 2023.

More than 10 Latin acts performed at Coachella in 2023.

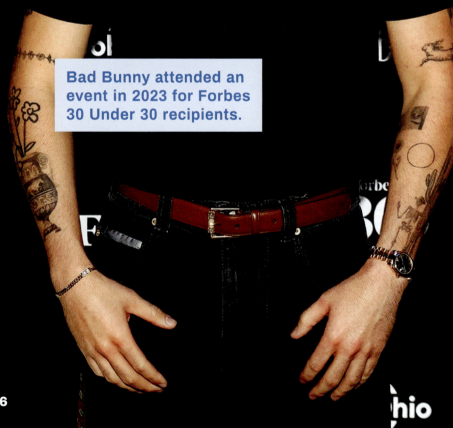

Bad Bunny attended an event in 2023 for Forbes 30 Under 30 recipients.

In October 2023, Bad Bunny released his fifth album. He called it *Nadie Sabe Lo Que Va a Pasar Mañana*. That means "Nobody Knows What Is Going to Happen Tomorrow." Once again, it topped the Billboard album chart. Bad Bunny was a true superstar.

SINGER AND SALESMAN

Bad Bunny sometimes does sponsorships. He helps companies sell their products. Examples include Cheetos and Pepsi. He has also worked with Adidas. He helped sell and design sneakers.

In the Spotlight

SOUNDS OF HOME

In *Un Verano Sin Ti*, Bad Bunny sings about home. He shares his love of summer in Puerto Rico. The songs include sounds of ocean waves and seagulls. Bad Bunny discusses love and hurt. He raps about human rights and feeling powerful.

Listeners loved the sounds and messages. In a short time, the album gained billions of streams on Spotify.

Un Verano Sin Ti was the most streamed album on Spotify in both 2022 and 2023.

Chapter 6

MANY SUCCESSES

Bad Bunny has fans all over the world. These fans have helped him set many records. For example, his songs are hugely popular on Spotify. He was Spotify's most-streamed artist for three years in a row. No other artist had done that.

Bad Bunny won Latin Artist of the Year at the 2023 Billboard Latin Music Awards.

In 2022, Bad Bunny appeared in *Bullet Train* with Brad Pitt (right).

Music is not Bad Bunny's only work, though. Over the years, Bad Bunny tried new things. He acted in TV shows and movies. He also became a professional wrestler. He co-owns a Puerto Rican basketball team. He owns a Florida restaurant, too. In 2023, he began Rimas Sports. This company helps athletes plan their careers.

Speaking out is important to Bad Bunny. He often talks about problems that Puerto Ricans face. One example is his song "El Apagón." It came out in 2022. A huge storm had hit Puerto Rico that year.

The storm caused massive damage. Many people lost power. Blackouts continued for weeks. Repair work was slow. Bad Bunny told how this harmed people. And at a 2022 concert, he criticized Puerto Rico's governor. He said leaders should do more to help.

Hurricane Fiona caused around $2.5 billion in damages in Puerto Rico.

In 2023, Bad Bunny (left) won a major award for raising awareness of LGBTQ issues.

Giving back is important to Bad Bunny, too. In 2018, he gave $100,000 to help children with disabilities in Puerto Rico. He also created the Good Bunny Foundation. This organization helps kids get into art, music, and sports.

GOOD GIFTS

Each year, the Good Bunny Foundation does a Christmas project. The organization gives out presents. Some are musical instruments. Others are supplies for arts or sports. Thousands of kids have received them.

FAST FACTS

Full name: Benito Antonio Martínez Ocasio
Birth date: March 10, 1994
Birthplace: Vega Baja, Puerto Rico

TIMELINE

1994 — Benito Antonio Martínez Ocasio is born on March 10.

2016 — The song "Diles" becomes a SoundCloud hit.

2018 — Bad Bunny releases his first album.

2020 — *El Último Tour del Mundo* is the first all-Spanish album to debut at No. 1 on the Billboard 200.

2022 — Bad Bunny is the first Latin act to have the top-selling tour.

2023 — Bad Bunny gives the first all-Spanish opening performance at the Grammy Awards.

COMPREHENSION QUESTIONS

Write your answers on a separate piece of paper.

1. Write a few sentences describing the main ideas of Chapter 6.

2. What fact about Bad Bunny did you find the most interesting? Why?

3. When did Bad Bunny's album *El Último Tour del Mundo* top the Billboard album chart?

    A. 2017
    B. 2020
    C. 2022

4. In which year did Bad Bunny release three albums?

    A. 2018
    B. 2020
    C. 2022

5. What does **sponsorships** mean in this book?

*Bad Bunny sometimes does **sponsorships**. He helps companies sell their products. Examples include Cheetos and Pepsi.*

    A. ads that show items to buy
    B. warnings against items
    C. flashy music videos

6. What does **milestone** mean in this book?

*The 2023 show was a **milestone**. It was the first to open with an all-Spanish performance.*

    A. something that had never happened before
    B. something that had happened many times before
    C. something that is just pretend

Answer key on page 64.

GLOSSARY

blackouts
When areas lose power.

collaborations
Songs that two or more people work on together.

disabilities
Limits or differences in a person's senses or movement.

freestyled
Made up the lyrics of a rap on the spot.

headlined
Performed as the main artist at an event.

industry
A group of companies that do similar work. For example, the music industry makes and sells music.

mainstream
Popular and known by many people.

manager
Someone who helps musicians plan their careers.

pandemic
A time when a disease spreads quickly around the world.

record labels
Companies that help artists put out music.

reggaeton
A style of music from Latin America that combines catchy rhythms with rap.

TO LEARN MORE
BOOKS

Abdo, Kenny. *Latin Music History*. Minneapolis: Abdo Publishing, 2020.

Rossiter, Brienna. *Great Careers in Music*. Mendota Heights, MN: Focus Readers, 2022.

Tieck, Sarah. *Puerto Rico*. Minneapolis: Abdo Publishing, 2020.

ONLINE RESOURCES

Visit **www.apexeditions.com** to find links and resources related to this title.

ABOUT THE AUTHOR

Rebecca Rowell has put her degree in publishing and writing to work as an editor and as an author, contributing to the creation of dozens of books. Recent topics as an author include the brands Gatorade and Nike and surviving being lost at sea. She lives in Minneapolis, Minnesota.

INDEX

acting, 53
awards, 4, 6, 23, 25, 37–38, 41

Cardi B, 20
Coachella, 44
concerts, 18–19, 37, 43, 54

DJ Luian, 16
Drake, 20

El Último Tour del Mundo, 35

Good Bunny Foundation, 57

J Balvin, 18, 20, 23

Las Que No Iban a Salir, 32
Latin trap, 26

Martin, Ricky, 41

Nadie Sabe Lo Que Va a Pasar Mañana, 47

Oasis, 23
Ozuna, 26

Puerto Rico, 8, 26, 48, 54, 57

reggaeton, 12, 16, 26, 37

Shakira, 28
SoundCloud, 12, 15
Spotify, 37, 48, 50
Super Bowl, 28

Un Verano Sin Ti, 38, 41, 48

X 100PRE, 23

YHLQMDLG, 31, 37

ANSWER KEY:
1. Answers will vary; 2. Answers will vary; 3. B; 4. B; 5. A; 6. A